D1453890

WHEN YOU **FAST...**

CONNECT   RECEIVE   ACHIEVE

WHEN YOU FAST . . .
CONNECT • RECEIVE • ACHIEVE

Unless otherwise noted, all Scripture quotations are taken from the King James Version of the Bible.

Scriptures marked (MSG) are taken from THE MESSAGE. Copyright © 1993, 1994, 1995, 1996, 2000, 2001, 2002. Used by permission of NavPress Publishing Group.

Scriptures marked (AMP) are taken from the Amplified® Bible, Copyright © 1954, 1958, 1962, 1964, 1965, 1987 by The Lockman Foundation. Used by permission. (www.Lockman.org)

Scriptures marked (NIV) are taken from the HOLY BIBLE, NEW INTERNATIONAL VERSION® copyright © 1973, 1978, 1984 by International Bible Society. Used by permission of Zondervan. All rights reserved.

Scriptures marked as (CEV) are taken from the Contemporary English Version Copyright © 1995 by American Bible Society. Used by permission.

Copyright © 2008 by Dr. David R. Williams

ISBN 0-938020-90-0

First Printed 2008

Published by:

MOUNT HOPE
CHURCH
Loving God . . . Loving You

Printed in the United States of America

OTHER BOOKS BY DAVE WILLIAMS

ABC's of Success and Happiness
Angels: They Are Watching You
Beatitudes: Success 101
The Beauty of Holiness
Coming Into the Wealthy Place
The Desires of Your Heart
Developing the Spirit of a Conqueror
Emerging Leaders
End-Times Bible Prophecy
Faith Goals
Filled
Genuine Prosperity
Gifts That Shape Your Life and Change Your World
Have You Heard From the Lord Lately?
How to Be a High Performance Believer
How to Help Your Pastor Succeed
The Jezebel Spirit
The New Life . . . The Start of Something Wonderful
Pacesetting Leadership
Private Garden
The Presence of God
The Pastor's Minute
Radical Fasting
Radical Forgiveness
Radical Healing
The Road to Radical Riches
Regaining Your Spiritual Momentum
Seven Sign-Posts on the Road to Spiritual Maturity
Somebody Out There Needs You
What to Do if You Miss the Rapture
The World Beyond
Your Pastor: A Key To Your Personal Wealth
36 Minutes With the Pastor

INTRODUCTION . . .

Each year, God has called Mount Hope Church to participate in a corporate fast. There are many physical and spiritual benefits to fasting, especially as we connect as a church family and encourage one another in getting the most out of our annual fast. Every year I look forward to this special time. As my body is cleansed from all the holiday feasting, I find that my spirit is freed to draw closer to God.

When I remove my attention from "feeding" my body, I am able to draw spiritual nourishment from more time spent in Bible study and intense times of prayer.

There are definite benefits to fasting, and if you want to learn more, please get a copy of my book Radical Fasting. The Hope Store also carries copies of The Miracle Results of Fasting. I know you will find both of them helpful. If you have already read them, I encourage you to review them.

I know that as you connect more directly to your Heavenly Father by focusing on Him, you will receive His direction for your walk in the coming year. I sincerely believe that as you are obedient in your participation, you will be led to walk in greater victory and achieve a closer, more dynamic relationship to His prompting through the Holy Spirit. Your life will catapult into the stratosphere of success!

Your friend and pastor,

Dave Williams

JANUARY 1

THE BIBLE

Pastor Bob Leroe of the Cliftondale Congregational Church in Saugus, Massachusetts told a story about a man who went to a bookbinder to get a well-worn New Testament rebound in leather. He wanted the side binding to read: "The New Testament." When the job was finished, the binder explained that he just wasn't able to get all the letters on the side, so he abbreviated: TNT.

Some people might like to imagine they can dilute this TNT by eliminating powder from the dynamite, but it's not possible to reduce God's Word. Comparing the Bible to TNT is certainly appropriate. The author of Hebrews describes the Scriptures as "powerful" and "sharper than any two-edged sword" (Hebrews 4:12).

We believe that the Bible, God's Inspired Word, is our guide for living. We base our decisions and set our priorities according to what is revealed in God's Word. To deny the divine origin of Scripture is to open the door to further unbelief, which is fatal to our spiritual lives. If we refuse to accept the Bible as our authoritative Word from God, any or all teachings of the Bible could be tossed overboard.

When Martin Luther was put on trial, he stated that he would gladly renounce his opinions if the prosecutors could show him where his views diverged from Scripture. "Prove me wrong from the Bible, and I'll gladly change," he asserted. The Scriptures—not man-made rules or tradition—were Luther's sole basis of authority. So, he declared to the Council, "Here I stand! I can do nothing else!"

In the Psalms (19 & 119), God's Word is compared to honey. It's the only food that does not spoil. Philosophies and trends will come and go, but the Word of God will always remain fresh, relevant, and true. If we hide its words in our heart, it will keep us from spoiling. Make sure you take your "Psalm Pilot" with you!

Mahatma Gandhi, a Hindu, knew the Bible contained TNT when he stated, "You Christians have in your keeping a document with enough dynamite to explode civilization, to turn society upside-down, to bring peace to this war-torn world. But you read it as if it were just good literature and nothing else."

Has the bookmark in your Bible moved lately? Let's take God's authoritative Word seriously. It deserves our trust because it is a book that has been shown to be reliable and relevant. It continues to inspire, challenge, comfort, instruct, guide, and bless its readers. Further, our response to its message has eternal consequences. Let's apply it to our lives this year and to following years to come. This book has the power to transform our lives!

JANUARY 2

NOT FORGOTTEN
A word from *Private Garden*

I have not forgotten you, My dear child. My eyes are on you and have been from the beginning of time. My Spirit has not ceased from His gentle work in your life. No My beloved, I have not forgotten you, and I never will.

You have everything to live for. Jesus died for you and was raised from the dead. My Spirit is working in you, on you, and through you. Everything good from My hand and My home is yours—including your wonderful, bright future. I am watching over you.

Yes, you face aggravations, trials of your faith, and even times of stumbling. I know how this makes you feel. But through it all, you have proven your faith is pure and genuine because you have kept going and continued to love by practice. You never saw Me, but you love Me and trust Me.

Oh, yes! Even the holy angels would give anything to be in your shoes! Chosen. Elected. Filled with the Spirit. Anointed. Crowned with the power of My Son through My Spirit. Oh, the victory—the blessed victory that is yours. Laughter, singing, and shouts of joy should rise up in you for the glorious gifts I have bestowed upon you.

Yes, My eyes are on you. I haven't forgotten you. I am the One who started a great work of art in you, and I will finish it. You are a masterpiece in the making.

Therefore, do not slip back into evil patterns—just doing what you feel like doing. You know better. Allow Me to continue to shape you, sand you, paint you, and fashion you after My Son Jesus. It was His sacred blood that bought you.

I haven't forgotten you. I'm still working in you. I am the source of your life, victory, success, and effectiveness.

I have given you a high calling as My instrument of harmony. I have accepted you, not rejected you. Remind yourself every day that I am for you, not against you. I remember your frame and issue mercy freely.

No, My dear one, I have not forgotten you!

JANUARY 3

THE BLESSING

One day, a woman came home to find her husband in the kitchen, shaking wildly with what appeared to be a wire running from his waist to an electric kettle. Intending to jolt him away from the deadly current, she whacked him with a nearby plank of wood by the back door, breaking his arm in two places. Until that moment he had been happily listening to his headphones.

Some days you just feel like you're walking under a curse.

Terrorist Khay Rahnajet, didn't pay enough postage on a letter bomb. It came back with "return to sender" stamped on it. Apparently he forgot it was a bomb. When he opened his letter, it blew him to bits. You may be thinking, "He deserved it!" And often when bad things happen, we are tempted to think we deserved it. But the truth is, because of your faith in Jesus, God has invoked a special blessing on your life.

If God Invokes A Blessing, No One Can Stop It.

> **"Praise the God and Father of our Lord Jesus Christ for the spiritual blessings that Christ has brought us from heaven!"**
>
> **— Ephesians 1:3 (CEV)**

God invoked a blessing on Abraham and promised that if anyone tried to curse him or his seed, the curser himself would receive a divinely invoked curse.

God blessed Job and gave him twice as much wealth as he ever had before his trouble.

We have the blessing of knowing we are chosen, accepted, and blameless before God, regardless of ourselves. It is based upon faith in Jesus Christ, God's Son. So always remember:

When God invokes a blessing, nobody can stop it.

JANUARY 4

GOSSIP

"My name is Gossip. I have no respect for justice. I maim without killing. I break hearts and ruin lives. I am cunning and malicious and gather strength with age. The more I am quoted, the more I am believed. I flourish at every level of society. My victims are helpless. They cannot protect themselves against me because I have no face. To track me down is impossible. The harder you try, the more elusive I become. I am nobody's friend. Once I tarnish a reputation, it is never the same. I topple governments, wreck marriages, and ruin careers—cause sleepless nights, heartaches, and indigestion. I spawn suspicion and generate grief. I make innocent people cry in their pillows. Even my name hisses. I make headlines and headaches."[1]

[1] Laura Schlessinger, *The Ten Commandments: The Significance of God's Laws in Everyday Life*, p. 203

JANUARY 5

18,355 YARDS OF PERSISTENCE

God has always honored persistence. I have always appre-
ciated Emmitt Smith. I was glad when he set the NFL rushing
record. He wasn't as flashy as Walter Payton or Barry Sanders,
and he never possessed true breakaway speed. His strength lay
in his ability to persist—he just kept running.

He ran for 18,355 yards. That's 10.2 miles! It took him 13
years to run only 10.2 miles. What's the big deal about that?
Well for one thing, he had 11 huge defensive players trying
to take off his head as he ran. Emmitt's average run over those
10.2 miles was 4.3 yards. That means he was tackled and
knocked down thousands of times. Do you know what he
did after every tackle? He got back up and ran the ball again.
Even though he was injured several times, he kept going. I'm
impressed that someone could be knocked down so many
times and still get up and run again, achieving greatness one
yard at a time.

Even the best of people get knocked down in life, but
what sets them apart from the quitters is that they get right
back up. Life is full of adversarial people who will tackle you.
You will face difficult circumstances that trip you up. The
poor widow in Jesus' parable had been knocked flat, but she
refused to stay down. She persisted in making her request to
the judge, and she finally won. So, never give up! Keep trying!
God will help you every step of the way.

JANUARY 6

OUR GREATEST NEED THIS YEAR

If our greatest need was for information, God would have sent an educator.

If our greatest need was for technology, God would have sent a scientist.

If our greatest need was for pleasure, God would have sent an entertainer.

If our greatest need was for money, God would have sent an economist.

However, since our greatest need is for mercy and forgiveness . . . God sent a Savior—only one—His precious Son Jesus.

JANUARY 7

DO YOU FEEL LIKE A FAILURE?

The next time you feel like a failure or unworthy or not forgiven, just remember...

Noah was a drunk.

Abraham was too old.

Isaac was a daydreamer.

Jacob was a liar.

Leah was ugly.

Joseph was abused.

Moses had a stuttering problem.

Gideon was afraid.

Sampson had long hair and was a womanizer.

Rahab was a prostitute.

Jeremiah and Timothy were too young.

David had an affair and was a murderer.

Elijah was suicidal.

Isaiah preached naked.

Jonah ran from God.

Naomi was a widow.

Job went bankrupt.

John the Baptist ate locusts.

Peter denied Christ.

The Disciples fell asleep while praying.

Martha worried about everything.

Mary Magdalene was a prostitute.

The Samaritan woman was divorced, more than once.

Zaccheus was too small in stature.

Paul was too religious.

Timothy had an ulcer.

Lazarus was dead!

Yet each of these people received extraordinary blessings from the Lord. You will also notice that each one of them did something unusual for the Lord as a result of their faith in Him.

You did something unusual when you gave your life to Jesus. And He made you an extraordinary individual when He put His life in you!

When You Fast . . .

What has God shown you this past week about success?

_____

_____

_____

_____

_____

_____

_____

_____

How can you apply God's success principals in your life?

_____

_____

_____

_____

_____

_____

_____

_____

JANUARY 8

THE MASTER KEY

Today, I will show you a master key to everything you could ever really want.

There are different keys for specific doors in our church building. I possess a master key that will open any of the doors. The master key will unlock any door in the building.

Did you know there is a Master Key to every problem, challenge, or situation you face that needs changing? That Master Key is the Presence of God.

In the presence of God, striving and struggling ends. In the presence of God, rest and peace comes and the struggle ceases.

God created all of humanity to have a deep, personal relationship with Him. God literally walked with Adam and Eve in the Garden of Eden. Think about that for a moment. Let it sink in. God walked and talked with Adam and Eve. They were able to completely enjoy His divine presence. God's desire for your life is to have that same kind of relationship with Him. He wants you to be able to walk in His presence.

Many Christians are completely ignorant of the presence of God. Even many ministers know nothing about the power of the presence of God. Anyone who has not experienced the power of God's presence is not justified to stand and talk about Him because such people don't know Him.

Perhaps that's why King David's greatest concern was losing the presence of God.

> **"Cast me not away from Your presence and take not Your Holy Spirit from me."**
>
> **—Psalm 51:11 (AMP)**

Brother Lawrence, who lived in the fifteenth century, was a lay brother in a Carmelite monastery. He is most often remembered for the closeness of his relationship to God as recorded in the classic Christian text, *The Practice of the Presence of God.* He said if there was one thing he could preach for the rest of his life, it would be practicing the presence of God.

Why not practice the presence of God today?

JANUARY 9

THE HIGH VALUE OF THE PRESENCE OF GOD

David, in his song of thanksgiving in 1 Chronicles 16, reveals four benefits to prioritizing God's presence: Splendor and majesty flow out from Him, strength and joy fill His place. Lift high an offering and enter His presence!

> **"Splendor and majesty flow out of him, strength and joy fill his place. Shout Bravo! to God, families of the peoples, in awe of the Glory, in awe of the Strength: Bravo! Shout Bravo! to his famous Name, lift high an offering and enter his presence! Stand resplendent in his robes of holiness!"**
>
> **—1 Chronicles 16:27-29 (MSG)**

What are the four benefits to your life when you practice the presence of God?

1. SPLENDOR—God will give you a shining supernatural beauty.
2. MAJESTY—This is honor or esteem. The presence of God is where your real esteem is imparted. You can fully understand your value only after experiencing the presence of God.
3. STRENGTH—This word means security, power, and might. He's got you covered, and you know it. You can be bold and fearless in every situation of life. When you've been in the presence of God,

you carry that presence with you into the office, the workplace, and on the streets.

4. JOY—This word includes gladness, ecstasy, and great happiness.

We could all benefit from splendor, honor, strength, and joy. These four reasons illustrate how practicing the presence of God is an amazing, daily opportunity for you.

JANUARY 10

I WANT TO CHANGE

I want to change.

Do YOU want to change?

It's not about changing others.

"True life changes come only through a partnership with God and begin by rejecting all self-centered change methods." James McDonald

"If I keep doing what I've always done, I'm going to keep getting what I've always gotten."

JANUARY 11

FAULTY METHODS OF TRYING TO CHANGE

Change your environment. Our problem is inside us, not around us.

Deal with your past; face up to it and let it go. God says the key to change is forgetting, not remembering. Ask God for the grace to forget your past. Your past does **not** determine your future.

Self-discovery—"I have to find myself." This is a pagan philosophy. People like to think they have the power to change themselves. What is troubling is the number of people professing Christ that have turned to pagan philosophies and ignore the transforming power of the Holy Spirit available to each of us.

The gospel is not about finding yourself, it's about losing yourself by letting go and letting God work in you.

- Faulty Method 1: Legalistic methods. Rules may produce an external change but can never change the heart. Legalism makes us unreal, hypocrites, phonies, and plastic. Genuine change by exterior rules is impossible.
- Faulty Method 2: Will suppression. When you say, "I won't do that. . ." you're more than likely going to do it, even though you don't want to.

The spirit is willing but the flesh is weak. It's about getting our wills to conform to God's will. Romans 7:18 talks about God working in you that which is good.

- Faulty Method 3: Endless Study. Many feel like they are a Dr. Jekyll and Mr. Hyde. Dr. Jekyll would feel ashamed of his hideous monster activities. When Dr. Jekyll changed from a sweet man to the criminal evildoer, Mr. Hyde, he would lament, "I can't believe that was inside me. I just cannot believe that I could live like that and do those things." Many times I've felt this way.

"I know better. How could I?" There is a great gulf between what we know and what we do (Romans 7:22-23).

Change can only come once we know that knowing just isn't enough.

JANUARY 12

KEYS TO REAL LIFE CHANGES

1. Admit and claim responsibility for being the problem. Paul was exhausted from trying to change himself (wretched—miserable as though exhausted from hard labor).
2. Turn to God everyday, because only He can change your heart.

> "The moment I decide to do good, sin is there to trip me up. I truly delight in God's commands, but it's pretty obvious that not all of me joins in that delight. Parts of me covertly rebel, and just when I least expect it, they take charge. I've tried everything and nothing helps. I'm at the end of my rope. Is there no one who can do anything for me? Isn't that the real question? The answer, thank God, is that Jesus Christ can and does. He acted to set things right in this life of contradictions where I want to serve God with all my heart and mind, but am pulled by the influence of sin to do something totally different."
>
> **—Romans 7:21-25 (MSG)**

He has begun a good work and has promised to complete it. God didn't drop down into your life to forgive you and then abandon you. He came to stay in your life. God started something in you and He's not going to give up on you until He sees the image of His Son in you and shining through you.

Remember, GOD STILL CHANGES PEOPLE!

JANUARY 13

REVOLUTIONIZE YOUR MARRIAGE

Son: "Dad, is it true? I heard that in ancient China, a man doesn't even meet his wife until after they marry!"

Father: "That happens everywhere, son, everywhere!"

There was a man who said, "I never knew what happiness was until I got married . . . and then it was too late!"

Today, after years of marriage, too many couples scarcely relate to each other. Many other activities, responsibilities, and interests seem to crowd out the importance of a happy marital relationship for millions of Americans.

Men want to be respected and women want to be loved; neither seems to be the case in most modern marriages.

This is what Paul wrote:

> "Honor Christ and put others first. A wife should put her husband first, as she does the Lord. A husband is the head of his wife, as Christ is the head and the Savior of the church, which is his own body. Wives should always put their husbands first, as the church puts Christ first.
>
> "A husband should love his wife as much as Christ loved the church and gave his life for it. He made the church holy by the power of his word, and he made it pure by washing it with water. Christ did this, so that he would have a glorious and holy church, without faults or spots or wrinkles or any other flaws.

> "In the same way, a husband should love his wife as much as he loves himself. A husband who loves his wife shows that he loves himself. None of us hate our own bodies. We provide for them and take good care of them, just as Christ does for the church, because we are each part of his body. As the Scriptures say, "A man leaves his father and mother to get married, and he becomes like one person with his wife." This is a great mystery, but I understand it to mean Christ and his church. So each husband should love his wife as much as he loves himself, and each wife should respect her husband."
>
> —Ephesians 5:21-33 (CEV)

Every couple can revolutionize their marriage by following these pointers.

Martin Luther once said, "Let the wife make the husband glad to come home; and let him make her sorry to see him leave."

Why not make this year the year to make your spouse glad he or she married you?

JANUARY 14

ARE YOU RESTING ENOUGH?

Several years ago, newspapers told how a new Navy jet fighter shot himself down. Flying at supersonic speed, he ran into cannon shells he had fired only a few seconds before. The jet was traveling too fast!

Our world has become the world of the Red Queen of Alice and Wonderland. "Now here, you see, it takes all the running you can do to keep in the same place. If you want to get somewhere else, you must run at least twice as fast as that."

Time magazine noted that back in the 60's, expert testimony was given to a Senate sub-committee on time management. They predicted that advances in technology would radically change how many hours a week people worked. They forecasted that the average American would be working 22 hours a week within 20 years. "The great challenge," the experts said, "would be figuring out what to do with all the excess time." Over 40 years later, after major advances in technology, how many of us are wondering what to do with all the excess time on our hands?

We seem to be always in a hurry. Yet, if we are to survive and thrive, we must ruthlessly eliminate hurry from our lives and learn to rest.

Without rest, we lose our zeal for life, find little pleasure, and accomplish less.

Without rest we become obsessed with work while our worship becomes sporadic and lazy. We feel consumed, over-extended, and even frantic.

Without rest, we lose our esteem and restlessly try to find it in work, achievement, and advancement.

Rest is vital to our spiritual lives.

Rest is imperative to our effectiveness.

Here's what Jesus said in Matthew:

> **"Are you tired? Worn out? Burned out on religion? Come to me. Get away with me and you'll recover your life. I'll show you how to take a real rest. Walk with me and work with me - watch how I do it. Learn the unforced rhythms of grace. I won't lay anything heavy or ill-fitting on you. Keep company with me and you'll learn to live freely and lightly."**
>
> **—Matthew 11:28-30 (MSG)**

Make this your year to honor the Sabbath principle of regular times of resting in the presence of Jesus.

Which devotional spoke most strongly to your heart? Why?

_____

_____

_____

_____

_____

_____

_____

_____

How do you plan to make changes in this area?

_____

_____

_____

_____

_____

_____

_____

_____

_____

JANUARY 15

ENTANGLEMENTS

Have you ever found your life tangled up in such a mess you felt like choking? It seems certain—that at one time or another—we've all found ourselves there.

One day, I heard a choking cry out in front of my house. I opened the door and there was my little white cockapoo tangled up in her chain. So, I led her around the shrubs, around the pillar, and around the porch until she was untangled. Then I let her in the house. Was she ever happy! She jumped up on me and howled almost as if she was saying "Thank you."

Then I thought about others who might be tangled up in a mess today. There's a Bible verse that, in a word picture, says this: "Jesus came to untangle the messes of life."

It's true. If you're in a mess today, God will untangle it if you'll let Him.

"He that loveth not knoweth not God; for God is love."

—1 John 4:8

"For the wages of sin is death; but the gift of God is eternal life through Jesus Christ our Lord."

—Romans 6:23

JANUARY 16

MAKING YOUR MARK ON LIFE

Let me ask you a personal question. Are you making a mark on your generation? Are you leaving the world something to remember you by? Now there's a thought. How will people remember you when you leave this life?

Stephen Grellet, a prominent Quaker missionary who died in New Jersey in 1855, left us something to remember him by. Following is an unforgettable short sermon he left us:

"I expect to pass through this world but once. Any good things, therefore, that I can do, any kindness that I can show a fellow being, let me do it now. Let me not defer or neglect it, for I shall not pass this way again."

Why not decide today to make your mark on this generation, and leave others something good to remember you by?

"You are the light of the world. A city that is set on a hill cannot be hidden. Nor do they light a lamp and put it under a basket, but on a lampstand, and it gives light to all who are in the house. Let your light so shine before men, that they may see your good works and glorify your Father in heaven."

—Matthew 5:14-16

"Verily, verily, I say unto you, He that believeth on me, the works that I do shall he do also; and greater works than these shall he do; because I go unto my Father."

—John 14:12

When You Fast . . .

"The steps of a good man are ordered by the Lord; and he delighteth in his way."

—**Psalm 37:23**

JANUARY 17

KEEP YOUR LIFE SIMPLE

I cleaned out my office the other day and was shocked to discover a hodge-podge collection of confusion stored undisturbed for over a decade! Do you want a good rule for success and happiness?

Keep your life simple.

Avoid disorder.

Discard the clutter.

Clean out your closet.

Trim down.

Give the stuff to the Salvation Army or Goodwill. They'll find a good use for it. If it's junk, throw it out.

Simplify and find order. It'll help you think better, feel better, and even perform better.

> **"Beloved, I wish above all things that thou mayest prosper and be in health, even as thy soul prospereth."**
>
> **—3 John 1:2**

> **"Peace I leave with you, my peace I give unto you: not as the world giveth, give I unto you. Let not your heart be troubled, neither let it be afraid."**
>
> **—John 14:27**

"But I fear, lest by any means, as the serpent be-
guiled Eve through his subtlety, so your minds should
be corrupted from the simplicity that is in Christ."

—2 Corinthians 11:3

JANUARY 18

ABC'S OF SUCCESS AND HAPPINESS

All of us desire happiness and success, don't we? Of course we do. And happiness and success are not merely a matter of talent, education, or skill. You and I both know plenty of un-educated, unskilled people who have achieved both happiness and success while others with phenomenal talent and educa-tion stand in the unemployment lines, even as we speak.

If talent and education alone cannot bring happiness and success, what can? Well, I sum it all up in what I call the ABC's of happiness and success.

A - Accept responsibility for your own life. Don't blame others.

B - Broaden your vision beyond the present.

C - Challenge yourself to reach higher than ever before.

D - Develop unswerving determination.

E - Exercise faith.

F - Forget the past.

G - Give God first place in your life.

Follow the ABC's and you'll discover overflowing success along with unquenchable happiness.

"Now faith is the substance of things hoped for, the evidence of things not seen,"

"But without faith it is impossible to please him: for he that cometh to God must believe that he is, and that he is a rewarder of them that diligently seek him."

—Hebrews 11:1, 6

"Brethren, I count not myself to have apprehended: but this one thing I do, forgetting those things which are behind, and reaching forth unto those things which are before."

—Philippians 3:13

"But seek ye first the kingdom of God, and his righteousness; and all these things shall be added unto you."

—Matthew 6:33

JANUARY 19

THE SIN OF MURMURING

Have you ever known a chronic murmurer? Have you ever met someone who continually tears others apart with words?

Murmuring means to complain, grumble, to evil-affect the minds of others toward someone else by offering inaccurate information or ungrounded complaints. It's like a gang of workers holding secret meetings, debating among themselves, and stirring up trouble for the boss.

They hurt the company, they hurt productivity, they hurt profits, and they hurt themselves. The Bible says murmuring brings disease to the heart and can bring devastating and disastrous consequences.

When someone tries to contaminate you with their murmuring gossip or gripes, you can stop them with five questions:

1. What's your reason for telling me this?
2. Where did you get your information?
3. Have you gone directly to the person?
4. Have you checked out the facts?
5. May I quote you if I check this out?

When murmurers realize that you're not going to allow your ears to become their garbage cans, they'll stop.

"Jesus therefore answered and said unto them, Murmur not among yourselves."

—John 6:43

"Grudge not one against another, brethren, lest ye be condemned: behold, the judge standeth before the door."

—James 5:9

JANUARY 20

HANDLING AN ATTACK

Have you ever been unfairly and falsely attacked? It is likely that you have experienced this in the past. Unfortunately, it is also likely that you will experience it again in the future. However, the way you deal with it could be different this year. Those who had called themselves friends had slandered King David, and this posed a threat to his good reputation. When he learned about the slander, he felt unspeakable distress and pounding at his heart. He felt drained. So how did he handle it?

First, he put his trust in God. You can never prove something you haven't done. An appeal to man is fruitless, so David appealed to God.

Second, he recognized this was an attack of an enemy, not a friend. One who slanders and gossips is nobody's friend.

Third, he didn't compromise on his innocence. He didn't boast about being perfect, but he wouldn't agree with his accusers either.

Fourth, he remembered the law of the boomerang: he who digs a pit for someone else will fall in it himself.

When you face an accusation, like we all do from time-to-time, do what David did. You'll come out on top.

"When they hurled their insults at him, he did not retaliate; when he suffered, he made no threats. Instead, he entrusted himself to him who judges justly."

—1 Peter 2:23 (NIV)

JANUARY 21

GOALS FOR THIS YEAR

People with clear goals accomplish 100 to 1000 times more than people without clear goals.

When Curtis Carlson founded the Gold Bond Stamp Company in Minneapolis at the age of 24, he also set a goal of earning $100 a week—a lofty sum during the Depression. He wrote down that objective and carried it in his pocket for years until the paper was frayed. Today, Carlson Companies rank among the nation's largest privately held corporations, with annual revenues topping $9 billion. This was a result of goals.

While Lee Iacocca was still in college, he set a goal of becoming vice president of Ford Motor Company before his 35th birthday. Seventeen years later, just 13 months after his self-declared deadline, it happened. This was the result of goals.

When the great architect, Frank Lloyd Wright, was asked at the age of 90 to single out his finest work, he answered, "My next one." Frank Lloyd Wright was ninety years old and still laying out goals.

Have you written down your goals in life? Can you articulate your mission in life in a sentence? Are you feeling burned out in areas of your life? Following St. Paul's example of writing down your objectives, purpose, and dreams would surely prove advantageous in the pursuing of—and successful completion of—your goals.

"Let your eyes look straight ahead, fix your gaze directly before you. Make level paths for your feet and take only ways that are firm. Do not swerve to the right or the left; keep your foot from evil."

—Proverbs 4:25-27 (NIV)

"I press on toward the goal to win the prize for which God has called me heavenward in Christ Jesus."

—Philippians 3:14 (NIV)

When You Fast . . .

What areas of your life are too complex?

_____

_____

_____

_____

_____

_____

_____

_____

What steps can you take to simplify your life?

_____

_____

_____

_____

_____

_____

_____

_____

_____

JANUARY 22

LIFE AFTER DEATH

There was an interesting article in *OMNI* magazine about Dr. Maurice Rawlings. Dr. Rawlings was a cardiologist who treated emergency patients repeatedly, many of whom have had near-death experiences.

It is not unusual for Dr. Rawlings to hear those people speak of seeing a bright light, lush green meadows, and rows of smiling relatives, along with a deep sense of peace. But he also said that nearly 50 percent of the near-death patients he interviewed spoke of fire and devil-like creatures and other horrible sights reflecting the darkness and terror of hell.

"Just listening to these patients has changed my whole life," claims Dr. Rawlings. "There is a life after death, and if I don't know where I'm going, then it's not safe to die."

Those are the words of the cardiologist who interviewed over 300 near-death patients who saw the world beyond.

Can you be sure of where you're going after this life is over? Is it safe for you to die? Jesus promised eternal life and Heaven for all those who trust in Him alone.

> **"Jesus saith unto him, I am the way, the truth, and the life: no man cometh unto the Father, but by me."**
>
> **—John 14:6**

> **"And as it is appointed unto men once to die, but after this the judgment: So Christ was once offered**

to bear the sins of many; and unto them that look for him shall he appear the second time without sin unto salvation."

—Hebrews 9:27-28

JANUARY 23

ENDLESS MERCY
A Word from *Private Garden*

My child, I have great news for you that you have almost forgotten. The news is this: I have benefits for you—many benefits. Remember My benefits, for I forgive all your sins and heal all your diseases. Yes, I am He who has surrounded you with tender mercies and loving care.

You have felt weak in yourself, but I am infusing My strength into your life as you wait upon Me. Your youth shall be renewed as an eagle's, and I will fill your life with good things from above. Do you think it is difficult for Me to bless you with inexhaustible benefits? Do you think it is hard for Me to seat you in heavenly places with Christ Jesus?

You have been treated unfairly in a particular situation. You know that. Some others know that. Most importantly, I know that. A root of bitterness has sought to establish itself within you for the purpose of destroying you completely by choking out My Word. But My mercy and My grace have been available to you non-stop.

Picture this: I have an endless supply of mercy, grace, and peace for you. When you are unforgiving, when you forget about My benefits, when you listen and believe lies instead of the truth, you cannot experience My supply. Now reach, My dear child, into My reservoir that you carry with you daily. Reach in deeply, and pull out My benefits. You will begin to realize that you *are* being lifted from strength to strength.

JANUARY 24

YOUR IMAGE OF GOD

Sadly, many people, even Christians, have a distorted image of God the Father. Satan and his demons are the great proliferators of error concerning God, the Father. Satan and his demons have a threefold plan:

1. To tempt
2. To deceive
3. To accuse

In order to accomplish all three of these evil plans, Satan just has to distort the image of the Father in your mind. It will then be easy to tempt, deceive, and accuse you. If he can pervert the image of God the Father in your thinking, he can accomplish his threefold goal in your life.

Since nobody has ever seen God the Father, it's easy for the devil to concoct his smear tactics against Him.

One of the errors we make is the mistake of viewing our relationship with the Father as merely a religious experience instead of an exciting family relationship. When you were born again, you were not born into a religion; you were born into a family, the family of God! God is now your Father and you are a son or daughter. It's so simple. Paul said,

> **"But I fear, lest by any means, as the serpent be-
> guiled Eve through his subtlety, so your minds should
> be corrupted from the simplicity that is in Christ."**
>
> **—2 Corinthians 11:3**

It's so simple, even a child can understand it. It doesn't take a great intellect or deep wisdom to be "born again" (although a person of great intellect or wisdom can be "born again"). Even a person who is mentally deficient can be "born again" because of the simplicity of the gospel.

By accepting Christ, you are translated out of Satan's kingdom, and born into God's family. You must now look to God as your heavenly Father and approach Him in a family manner, not a religious manner.

When you come as a family member, you can have faith for great gifts from God because you understand He loves and cares about you. He's not up there just sitting behind His judge's bench, waiting to flatly say "no" to every request you make. He is your Father. You can go right into the family room.

"In my Father's house are many mansions . . . ."

—John 14:2

In the original language this Scripture says, "In my Father's house are many rooms." Envision yourself in the family room sitting by the fireplace with God, your Father. Close your eyes. Relax and enjoy your time chatting with Him.

God is more interested in a family-like relationship with you than a religious experience.

51

JANUARY 25

BOUNDARIES

The Old Covenant seemed to be full of boundaries, rules, do, don'ts, and demands. Under our New Covenant, God still has boundaries for us, but He doesn't want us to feel like we're always on "thin ice" around Him.

When my children were young, one of the boundaries in our home was my lower level office. I had bookcases, books, tapes, a gigantic desk, and various other office equipment and supplies. We observed a rule in our home that "you don't come down and bother Daddy when he's studying or working." I liked to get into the flow of things when I was studying and didn't want to be disturbed.

Occasionally though, I would hear little footsteps on the stairs. Glancing up from my work, I would see my children peeking around the corner, with awkward, guilty looks on their faces.

"Daddy, can we work down here with you?"

They didn't want anything but to be in my presence. I usually forgot about the boundary and just enjoyed that relationship with them. Sometimes they would play quietly by themselves while I was working. They didn't want anything from me. They simply wanted to be with me. It blessed me.

And it blesses your Father in heaven when you want to be in His presence. The Bible says,

"...In thy presence is fullness of joy..."

—Psalm 16:11

At times, I'll plug in a praise CD and just worship God and enjoy His presence.

He's not a grouchy old character, but a loving, heavenly Father who loves me, wants me to succeed, and desires that I be fruitful in life. You should try it sometime. Remember, we are not part of a religion; we are part of a family. God is the Father, and we are all brothers and sisters.

Enjoy His presence today!

JANUARY 26

PRAYER HEARD
A Word from *Private Garden*

My precious child, I have heard your prayer; I have listened to your plea. I will never turn away from you—you can count on that. Even when you feel as though you are not able to "break through," I am bending My ear to hear your words, and I will answer based upon your faith.

Do not believe the lies of your enemy. Do not trust the changing emotions you feel. Trust only in My Word and in My Son Jesus, and you will certainly see quick answers to your prayers. But if you try to control the situations, manipulate the outcomes, you will enter a wilderness experience and have no real sense of My presence in your life.

I do not reject your pleas, My little one. I have listened, and continue to listen, as you cry out to Me even in your heart. I will appear, and I will rebuild that which sin, and the enemy, has torn apart. I have heard your groaning. Remember the heavens are the work of My hands. You think only of earthly things, but the earth is minuscule compared to the place I am preparing for you.

I am the God of all Creation: the solar systems, the galaxies, the quasars, and My home—which is beyond where the human eye can see. I have looked from heaven to earth. Now, My dear child, look from earth to heaven. My Son Jesus bridged the gap when He died for you and was raised for your justification. There is so much—so much—that you do not know.

Trust Me, I will not cut you down at this point in your life. I will not allow you to perish at the hands of My enemies. I have ordained you to thrive in My presence and to live in My security with My peace. Even when it seems as though multitudes have gathered against you, I will not let you perish. They shall perish, and you shall remain.

JANUARY 27

WHAT IS MY CALLING?

Do you know what you're called to do on this earth? Do you ever feel frustrated in your calling or that it is not leading you anywhere? Do you feel like you're working hard but coming up short? Are you easily burned out, or have such a busy schedule that you hardly know whether you're coming or going?

Have you ever asked, "What is my calling in life?"

Many people struggle with their calling.

There was an old southern preacher who had little training; but he preached his heart out, and the people in his church knew he loved God. He touched many lives with his messages. One day, the seminary sent a student to preach at his church. The student walked up to the podium, threw his Bible open, and in a very smug manner presented an oratory that had no theological or grammatical flaws. Neither did it have any relevance. His message confused the church as they searched for the meaning in it. When this arrogant young preacher concluded, the old southern preacher went up and said, "Son, were you sent, or did you just went?"

That old preacher knew the difference between being called and being driven! That young man was driven to excel as an academic, and may have had superior knowledge and training. However, what was it worth if he was pursuing his calling in the wrong direction?

The first subject Paul touched on in his letter to the Romans was "calling." If you and I don't understand calling, we won't be equipped to glorify our Lord or to please Him completely. In fact, we may find ourselves "driven" in the wrong direction and living unfruitful lives.

Paul started his letter like this:

> **"Paul, a servant of Jesus Christ, called to be an apostle, separated unto the gospel of God."**
>
> **—Romans 1:1**

Notice that the second and third words of this letter are "a servant." It seems Paul couldn't wait to declare it, so he put it right up front.

Why was he so eager? Because he knew a secret: The first calling of every Christian is servanthood.

If you struggle with your call and wonder when it will "kick in," perhaps you haven't realized that before you do anything great or lasting, you have to become a servant.

In using this term servant, or bond slave, of his own position to Christ, Paul was saying, "I love Jesus Christ and I'm going to serve Him because I want to, not because I have to." And there we have the first key to a successful calling—voluntarily submitting to the call of servanthood. You see, the second thing Paul was called to was apostleship, but that wasn't his choice to make. The path to apostleship ran through servanthood. He didn't become a Christian and decide one day to be an apostle. No, he first fell before the Lord and agreed to be a servant, and then the Lord called him to apostleship.

A pastor was talking with a man who was about to join his church. The man explained, "I want to join the church because I want to be fed." The pastor replied, "Well, that's fine, but we all would be better off if you would take off your bib and put on an apron!"

Find your calling in life by beginning to serve in some capacity.

JANUARY 28

SOMETHING TO THINK ABOUT

Somebody left a poem on my desk one time that read:

I dreamed death came the other night,
and Heaven's gates swung wide.
With kindly grace,
an angel ushered me inside.

There to my astonishment stood folks
I had known on earth.
Some I had judged and labeled
unfit or of little worth.

Indignant words rose to my lips
but never once set free.
For every face showed stunned surprise—
No one expected me!

When You Fast . . .

What call has God placed on your life?

_____

_____

_____

_____

_____

_____

_____

_____

_____

How are you answering His call?

_____

_____

_____

_____

_____

_____

_____

_____

_____

JANUARY 29

LITTLE FOXES
A Word from *Private Garden*

Abide in Me, and let My Word abide in you. Herein am I glorified that you bear much fruit. I know you have desired to be productive and fruitful; yet you have resisted My gentle pruning. My child, I only prune for your benefit so that you might come into the abundance I have decreed for your life. You ask, "When have I resisted?" I answer, "In your associations and practices." If you love Me, obey Me.

Allow Me to prune away those things that hinder and weigh you down. Let me remove those weights that slow you down; let me remove those things that seem important, but only serve to provide roadblocks to your progress. I am for you, not against you. Trust Me when I do My pruning, cleansing work in you. I am cutting away those unprofitable things and associations so that you may come into greater abundance, and I will be more greatly glorified.

Some sins seem so little; but little "foxes" can spoil the vine. Even as vines exist to bring forth juicy, sweet fruit, so do you, as a branch on the "vine," exist to bring forth fruit. Little branch, abide in the Vine—My Son Jesus. Please remember, no matter how painful the pruning is, I have a very specific purpose in mind—to give you better quality and greater quantity of fruit in abundance.

Let My pruning season drive you to depend on Me. Let Me remove those things that keep you from becoming all I have intended. If a vineyard isn't pruned, it becomes worthless. You are My precious branch in the Vine. Therefore, trade the unimportant for My best. As you allow Me to trim these hindrances from your life, I will keep you from hazards and infections. I will bring you into a greater abundance than you thought possible.

Abide in My Word; it is My pruning tool. Feed yourself with the nutrients of My Word, and you will bear fruit in season and out—far more and far superior fruit to those who refuse My pruning work.

JANUARY 30

JESUS TOOK THE RAP

The story is told about a king who made a law that anyone caught stealing would be whipped forty lashes at the whipping post. One night, police arrested a little 77-year-old lady for stealing, and word got back to the King that it was his own mother. There was no way her body would be able to take forty lashes. She'd be dead after the third one.

The next day the crowds began to gather at the coliseum. They had heard someone was caught stealing, and they wished to see the beating. The whipping post was put up in the center of the arena. Thousands of people from the kingdom were gathered around to see if the king was going to execute his justice. The whip master cracked the whip in the air. It sounded like a gunshot echoing around the coliseum.

The king's mother was brought out, hands bound. Everyone was breathless as the whip master began to lift his whip to take his first stroke, but then the king's voice rang out, "Stop!" The whip master held his lash. The king stepped out of his royal booth, walked down into the coliseum, ripped off his royal attire, stripped off his shirt, put his body around his mother and said, "Go ahead and whip." He received the forty lashes for her, and both justice and mercy were executed.

That's what Jesus did for us. He not only took the rap for us, He took the wrath for us. Only our faith in Him alone will save us

JANUARY 31

MAKING PLANS

A man came to me one day and asked, "Brother Dave, how do you plan? Do you have any books that can teach me how to make plans?"

God Himself has always worked by plans. He has a plan for salvation, a plan for peace and joy, a plan for each individual's life. He even has a blueprint for the earth and the ocean.

> **"I was there when He made the blueprint for the earth and the oceans."**
>
> **—Proverbs 8:29 (TLB)**

Planning is a vital stage to any project. If you fail to make plans, you'll quickly discover that circumstances, situations, problems, and other people will begin to determine your priorities. This will leave you frustrated at the end of the day, with a feeling that you've made no real accomplishments.

Author Louis A. Allen states, "The greatest source of long-term failure for organized endeavors, undoubtedly, is the failure to plan."

If you are looking for failure, then simply neglect to make solid plans. The failure to make sound plans will assure you of an unsuccessful project. The downfall of 98% of all the projects that failed was their lack of proper planning.

You wouldn't consider building a house without a blueprint. Why start a project without a plan? Why try to make your God-given dreams come true without a plan for doing it?

Studies have proven that the more time we spend in advance planning for a project, the less total time is required for it.

One of the most productive things we can do with our time is use it to prayerfully plan. Plan your day, plan your week, plan your years, plan your business, plan your ministry, plan to see your dreams coming true . . . counting on God to direct you.

PRAY FOR YOUR PASTOR

Pray for your pastor and his family daily. This seems elementary, yet it's surprising how many members don't even mention their pastor in prayer one day in any given week.

Two particular times your pastor needs special and intense intercession are the day before he ministers and the day after. The day before he ministers is often a time when distractions come to divide his attention. The phone may ring non-stop, "drainers" may stop by to chat about nothing in particular or the enemy may harass his family. On the day after he ministers, often depression will tempt him. If twenty people came to Christ he'll wonder why it wasn't thirty. He'll recall all of his mistakes, feeling that he should have done better or that more people ought to have been in church.

Pray for his and his family's protection. Use Psalm 91 as a guide, and as you pray include your own family.

Specific things to pray for your pastor include:

- Give thanks for his calling and gifts
- That he'll be blessed with a rich study time in preparation for ministry
- That he'll be shielded from the fear of man
- That he'll possess sound leadership wisdom
- That the Lord will anoint him with apostolic results of signs, wonders, miracles, and revelation

- That God will honor him with lasting fruit from his labors
- That God will cancel any satanic assignments against him
- That all obstacles to his ministry will be removed
- Rebuke all distractions from his devotional life
- Claim the Scriptural promises of protection over him
- Bind any hindering and manipulating spirits in your pastor's life
- Loose the forces of Heaven to aid your pastor in prayer and ministry
- Expect great things in the services led by your pastor

Listen to the Holy Spirit for other areas of intercession for your pastor, especially during these special times of fasting and prayer.

FEBRUARY 2

THE PRAYER OF JABEZ FOR MY PASTOR

Lord, bless my pastor . . .
In his home
In his ministry
In his personal life
In his times of study and preparation
In his speaking and preaching assignments and in his travels

Put your hand upon my pastor . . .
Anoint him powerfully
To do more than he can do alone
To achieve more than he can achieve
To see results in his ministry that are supernatural
To touch people's lives in a unique way
To minister in an unforgettable way

Enlarge my pastor's territory . . .
Personally and in his ministry
In his influence among common people
In his influence among ministers
In the distribution of his books
In his effect upon millions of lives
In his preaching and teaching ministry
In our church
In the Soul Zone
Prosper my pastor in every way

Keep my pastor from all evil . . .
People with ill motives
Wicked people with evil designs
Gossiping tongues and rumor-mongers
Hold him close and protect him from any plan of the devil
In thoughts, words, and deeds

Help my pastor to never cause hurt . . .
To himself
To his family
To his church
To fellow believers
To fellow ministers
To the Body of Christ in general

Thank you, Lord, for hearing this prayer for my pastor,
and for answering it and blessing me for interceding.

FEBRUARY 3

GROWING UP SPIRITUALLY

Spiritual babies are carnally minded, typically acting with envy, and whining often about many things. In my book, *Growing Up in Our Father's Family*, I give the reader the signs of spiritual babyhood:

- Babies are always dependent upon others. Someone has to change them, feed them, and do things for them all the time. Spiritual babies require constant attention and will be sure to behave in such a way as to get it.
- Everything goes into a baby's mouth. My daughter would eat dirt, crayons, bugs, and anything she could fit into her mouth. Spiritual babies are always taste-testing the new doctrines and fads that blow through town.
- Babies are jealous. Spiritual babies wonder why someone else was selected for the leading role in the Easter play. They mutter words like this: "Why did the pastor visit Mr. Jones? He never visited me."

St. Paul also talked about spiritual children. They aren't babies, but neither are they spiritually mature.

> "That we henceforth be no more children, tossed
> to and fro, and carried about with every wind of doc-
> trine, by the sleight of men, and cunning craftiness,
> whereby they lie in wait to deceive;
>
> "But speaking the truth in love, may grow up into
> him in all things, which is the head, even Christ"
>
> —Ephesians 4:14-15

These verses speak of spiritual children as being unstable and having problems with their mouths.

- Children are naturally curious, nosey, and snoopy. They always have their noses in someone else's business.
- Children talk endlessly. A baby becomes a child when the nonstop talking begins. Spiritual children often gab excessively about something, someone, or some situation.
- Children are always trying to make an impression on someone. Spiritual children often say things like, "Look at this car the Lord gave me. It cost me $40,000, but it hauls my new boat just fine."
- Children are know-it-alls.
- Children have a habit of fighting with their brothers and sisters.
- Children are unreliable.
- Children are essentially undisciplined and unorganized in everyday practical matters.

What does a believer need for proper spiritual growth into mature adulthood?

- **Proper diet**. Feast on the Word of God and good, solid teaching (1 Peter 2:2).
- **Proper exercise**. Exercise your faith, your service, your witness, your testimony (read Ephesians 4:14-16 in the Amplified Bible).
- **Proper rest**. That is, resting in Jesus' finished work (Matthew 11:28; Hebrews 4:9-10).

FEBRUARY 4

SO SIMPLE
A Word from *Private Garden*

You have noticed many times, My dear child, how fickle people attempt to make something of their lives while leaving Me in the shadows. They work hard, with great effort and intensity, but down the road they find their attempts have been futile. You have seen it, and even had a tinge of envy for their lifestyle.

But listen to Me, My beloved child. Whenever people give priority to matters that are outside of My priorities, their dreams become mere illusions. They end up settling for less than My pre-planned best for them. Pursuing self-will, they end up finding only futility, frustration, and emptiness. Their lives become divided instead of multiplied.

They do not see themselves as idolatrous; they will not admit that I am not in first place in their lives. Nonetheless, all their work, ambition, and motivation leads them only to meaninglessness and vexation. Soon they lose interest in the high and holy things on My heart. The excitement they felt for My gifts and promises dies within them.

Too late, they discover all their wasted years. Their scheming and grasping for more comes to an end; their dreams are long gone. Like a fish caught in a net, they see no way out as hard as they try to escape.

But to you I am giving this advance notice to warn you of the sidetracks you must avoid to be fully all you are called to be.

Honor Me. Enjoy Me. Man's life, as precious and beautiful as it may be, is soon over.

As Solomon concluded, "Fear God and do what He tells you." It's so simple, My dear child. Reverence Me. Obey Me. For I have grand designs to fulfill in you and through you. But it cannot be a work of your flesh. It must be a gentle, powerful work of My Spirit.

Yes, I love you, and I long to walk and talk with you in My secret garden where there is an overflowing abundance of fruit and special gifts for you. I want your heart to be bursting with joy—full and overflowing.

Put your full weight upon Jesus; cast all your cares and anxieties on Him, because He cares deeply for you. Avoid illusions and fantasies. Make My priorities the top priorities in your life, and you will bear much fruit wherein I shall be glorified.

Are you spiritually mature? What areas do you need to change?

_____

_____

_____

_____

_____

_____

_____

_____

_____

What actions can you take to grow and mature spiritually?

_____

_____

_____

_____

_____

_____

_____

_____

_____

FEBRUARY 5

REFUSE THE VICTIM MENTALITY

Somebody asked Winston Churchill what most prepared him to lead Great Britain through World War II. Churchill replied, "It was the time I repeated a class in grade school." The inquirer probed, "You mean you flunked a grade?" Churchill responded, "I never flunked in my life. I was given a second opportunity to get it right."

Reframing a situation is one way to prevent the success-draining attitude of a victim. Churchill reframed his history by taking a negative situation and turning it into a positive learning opportunity.

Life can shovel dirt on us at times. But at all costs, we must refuse to develop a victim's mentality. The victim mentality is a death rattle to effectiveness and fruitfulness.

One day a farmer's donkey fell down into a well. The animal cried piteously for hours as the farmer tried to figure out what to do. Finally, he decided the animal was old and the well needed to be covered up anyway. It just wasn't worth it to retrieve the donkey. For that reason, he invited all his neighbors to come over and help him. They all grabbed a shovel and began to shovel dirt into the well. At first, the donkey realized what was happening and cried horribly. Then, to everyone's amazement, he quieted down. A few shovel loads later, the farmer finally looked down the well and was astonished at what he saw. With every shovel of dirt that hit his back, the donkey was doing something amazing. He would shake it off and take a step up. The donkey continued this plight with each heap of dirt that came his way. Before long, everyone was amazed as the donkey stepped up over the edge of the well and trotted off!

Moral: Life will undoubtedly heap loads of dirt on you. The trick to getting out of the well is to shake it off and take a step up. Each trouble, every bit of resistance is a stepping-stone. We can find our way out of the deepest wells with perseverance and by refusing defeat!

Shake it off and take a step up!

DON'T THINK TOO HIGHLY OF YOURSELF

A group of travelers were made to wait for their airplane, which was late due to the flight cancellation of another flight. The crowd looked ornery and impatient as the time went on and on. Finally an angry passenger pushed his way to the front of the line, slammed his ticket down and said, "I must be on this flight now and I must be in first class." The flight attendant, remaining pleasant, responded, "Sir, we will get to you as soon as possible, but you must wait in line like everyone else." He quickly countered, "Ma'am, do you have any idea who I am?" Without hesitation, she smiled, picked up her intercom microphone and said, "We have a passenger here at the gate who does not know who he is. If anyone can help him find his identity, please come to gate 17."

Do you know the Beatles' song from the sixties entitled, "I'm a loser"?

In this recording the Beatles sing,

> What have I done to deserve such a fate
> I realize I have left it too late
> And so it's true, pride comes before a fall
> I'm telling you so that you won't lose all
> I'm a loser and I'm not what I appear to be

Actually, the Beatles were paraphrasing a Bible verse that reads, "Pride goes before destruction and a haughty spirit before a fall." Pride and haughtiness make a person a real loser. I'm not talking about being proud of your family, your job, your church, or your community. I'm talking about the kind of pride that says, "I'm better than you, or smarter than you, or I have more than you."

St. James tells us that God resists the proud, but gives favor to the humble. Simply put, if we want to stay on top, we can't allow arrogance to rule. It involves realizing that everything we have started with is a gift from God, even though we may have developed that gift. It entails realizing God is God and I'm not.

The Beatles were right. Pride comes before a fall and turns people into losers. Humility comes before promotion and turns people into winners.

FEBRUARY 7

SUCCESS OR FAILURE?

How do we know when we look at a person's life if that person is a success or a failure? It is often difficult to predict.

There was a ditsy redhead on television years ago. Many of us grew up watching her. Her name was Lucille Ball.

Lucy had been only a minor movie star, but the new medium of television was a perfect showcase for her talents. Subsequently, at the age of forty, Lucille Ball became a major star.

Thirty-five million Americans each week tuned in to watch this delightful featherhead botch up situation after situation. Off-screen, however, Lucille Ball was a clever business woman. With the help of her husband, Desi Arnaz, she turned her TV career into an empire. They recorded each episode on film in order to preserve it for future sales. It was a smart move. In America, I Love Lucy reruns have been seemingly ongoing. The same thing has happened in other countries as they have opened up their airwaves. At one time, Lucy was on screen somewhere in the world every minute of the day.

Lucy became so powerful, she bought a movie studio, RKO. Some of you can remember when a major share of TV programs were produced by Desilu Productions. No movie star could match the power of Lucille Ball.

Incidentally, when Lucille Ball began studying to be an actress in 1927, she showed very little potential. She was told by the head instructor of the John Murray Anderson Drama School, "Try another profession. Any other."

Sometimes you just can't see success even when it's right in front of your face.

To the unbelieving world, Jesus failed.

To the believing world, it was the greatest success story in all of history.

The devil believed he thought it up, but God used him as a stooge in His amazing plan to save lost souls and bring them into fellowship with Himself.

FEBRUARY 8

THE TOP 10 WAYS TO TURN OFF YOUR KIDS TO CHURCH

I'm grateful we don't experience this type of thinking in our congregation; however it's always wise to examine ourselves to make certain our church family is not taking part in the following:

1. Schedule personal or family events to conflict with church services and activities.
2. Don't get too close to anyone in church. Refrain from developing relationships with Christians lest your children learn the joy and benefits of fellowship with other believers.
3. Look often at your watch during worship and complain bitterly, look annoyed, or freak out when church lasts longer than you think it should.
4. Tithe and financially support your church and its missions with the same enthusiasm you pay taxes.
5. Do the best you can to make sure the kids arrive on time to soccer lessons and school events, but don't worry if they miss or are late to church.
6. Bring your family to church only when:
   a) You have nothing better to do

    b) You have a personal need

    c) You feel really guilty

7. Don't volunteer for anything or make any kind of long-term commitment at church. Remember, you've got to keep your options open to do things that are more important.

8. Change churches every few years.

9. Remind your kids how imperfect your church leaders are and regularly point out their mistakes.

10. Whatever you do, don't let church influence the way you live your life.

FEBRUARY 9

COCKROACHES, SPARROWS, AND EAGLES

I was reading a devotional by Harold Salas, which said that people can be likened to one of three creatures spoken of in the Bible. It's our choice which one we most closely resemble. Here are their characteristics:

The first and most lowly creature is the cockroach. Cockroaches are everywhere in dark and hidden places. They are plentiful, intrusive, and always trying to get into something that doesn't belong to them and ruin it. They don't achieve anything; they are never helpful or selfless; but generally they survive.

The second creature is the sparrow. When you see a cockroach you say, "Ick." When you see a sparrow you say, "Oh." Sparrows don't merely survive, they are successful. They fly around, but never fly very high. They play it safe, take care of their own business, and thus they are common and ordinary. They never achieve greatness.

The third creature is the mighty eagle. When you see an eagle, you say "Wow! Look at that." An eagle flies high, has far-seeing vision, and extraordinary grace. Because it has great vision and power, it can cover more ground, take in more territory, and achieve greatness. An eagle spreads its wings and effortlessly soars on thermal currents wherever God's hand moves him. An eagle not only survives and is successful, an eagle is significant. They are uncommon.

A mother, when she was angry, would say, "I love you because you are my child, but right now I don't like you very much!" I think God must think that about us at times. He loves us, but sometimes our thoughts, actions, and attitudes must grieve him. He wants each one of us to soar like the eagle, not creep like a cockroach, or flit like a sparrow.

When you leave this life, how will you be remembered? As a cockroach, a sparrow, or an eagle? When you enter Heaven will you hear, "Well done!"? Or, will you hear, "Oh, it's you. Come in I guess."? I'm praying that I hear the first. How about you?

In this devotional, you have been asked to think about many aspects of your life and Christian walk. I pray that during this fast, God has given you direction and spoken to your heart about areas you need to work on. I pray that this 40-day fast has benefited you spiritually and physically, and that you are off to a strong start in the new year!

CONTACT INFORMATION

Mount Hope Church and International Outreach Ministries
202 S. Creyts Road
Lansing, Michigan 48917

For a complete list of Dave Williams' life-changing
books, CDs and videos call:

Phone: 517-321-2780
800-888-7284
TDD: 517-321-8200

or go to our web site:
www.mounthopechurch.org

For prayer requests, call the
Mount Hope Global Prayer Center
24 hour prayer line at:
517-327-PRAY
(517-327-7729)

This devotional was excerpted from previously published books by Pastor Dave Williams, including:

Faith Goals

The ABC's of Success and Happiness

The Desires of Your Heart

Pacesetting Leadership

For more information and a complete list of titles available from Decapolis Publishing, please use the contact information found on the preceding page.